SWAN FLYWAY
The Tundra Swan

SMITHSONIAN
WILD HERITAGE COLLECTION

For Jesse
    — D. L.

For Andria Leger Cassidy
    — J. B.

Copyright © 1993 by Trudy Management Corporation,
165 Water Street, Norwalk, CT 06856, and Smithsonian Institution,
Washington, DC 20560.

First Edition
10 9 8 7 6 5 4 3 2 1
Printed in Singapore

Library of Congress Cataloging-in-Publication Data

Limpert, Dana. 1959-

Swan Flyway : the tundra swan / by Dana Limpert :
illustrated by Jo-Ellen Bosson.
        p.   cm.
Summary: A family of tundra swans migrate from Chesapeake Bay to their
Canadian summer home, where they raise five new cygnets before once again
making the difficult journey back to their winter home by Thanksgiving Day.
        ISBN 0-924483-95-4
1. Tundra swan — Juvenile fiction. [1. Tundra swan — Fiction.
2. Swans — Fiction.] I. Bosson, Jo-Ellen. 1941- ill. II. Title.
        PZ10.3.L635Sw 1993
        (Fic) — dc20   92-42381
                                                                    CIP
                                                                    AC

SWAN FLYWAY

The Tundra Swan

by *Dana Limpert*

Illustrated by Jo-Ellen Bosson

Soundprints
A Division of Trudy Management Corporation
Norwalk, Connecticut

Spring arrives with a gentle March breeze, warming the waters of a bay called Chesapeake. The waters are growing *too* warm for the tundra swans that winter in the bay.

"Honk." Mother and father swan call to their eight-month-old cygnets. "Honk." It is time to show them the way to their summer home on the Canadian tundra.

Father swan pumps his powerful wings just above
the water — webbed feet slapping the surface. He
rises into the air, and mother swan and the cygnets
follow. Other swan families join them. Then, led by
father swan, the flock forms a long V-shape and
turns north. Their spring migration has begun.

The journey is not easy. High over Pennsylvania's hills the flock flies into a terrible storm. Strong winds make it hard to fly. Rain beats at the swans in a sky lit by lightning. Father swan leads the flock to safety on a sheltered lake along their flyway. They stay until the storm ends. And they are content because the lake is full of the underwater plants they like to eat.

9

After the storm they take off again. Across the Great Lakes and the forests of Canada they fly, stopping often at lakes or ponds for food and rest. At night they sleep upon the open water with their heads tucked under their wings. If it is cold, they stay for a while. But if it is warm, instinct urges them to move on quickly, for the ice-bound plants of the north are reachable again.

Weeks pass. The May sun is thawing
snow and ice into meltwater pools as the
flock arrives on the tundra.

The cygnets are now 10 months old and ready to care
for themselves. Mother and father swan leave them with
a flock of young tundra swans where they will be safe.
Then the pair flies to a raised hummock on the lake.

By June the icy tundra is a grassland tundra — with puffs of cottongrass and tufts of poppies. Using mosses, sedges and grasses, mother and father swan build a snug nest on the hummock.

In the nest mother swan lays five white eggs and keeps them warm. Father swan takes his turn warming the eggs, too, so mother swan can feed.

Hungry, she enters the water. Up tips her tail as she stretches her long neck to reach the tasty plants that grow on the lake bottom.

Suddenly father swan trumpets a warning from
the nest! Another tundra swan has wandered too close.
Father swan raises his wings and chases the intruder
away with a flurry of feathers and feet.

Late in June the sun shines both day and night. One by one, five new cygnets peck their way out of the eggs in the nest. Within a day, they are paddling through the water. But they stay close and listen to their parents' calls.

Mother and father swan show the cygnets where to find underwater plants that are good to eat. But the cygnets' short necks cannot reach the most tender vegetation. And so their parents help, scraping the plants up off the bottom.

22

23

24

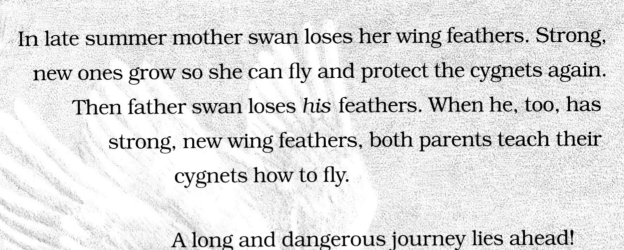

In late summer mother swan loses her wing feathers. Strong, new ones grow so she can fly and protect the cygnets again. Then father swan loses *his* feathers. When he, too, has strong, new wing feathers, both parents teach their cygnets how to fly.

A long and dangerous journey lies ahead!

One frosty, fall morning snow swirls from the sky and a familiar urge stirs deep within the tundra swans. It is time to leave their summer home — before ice freezes the foods of the tundra.

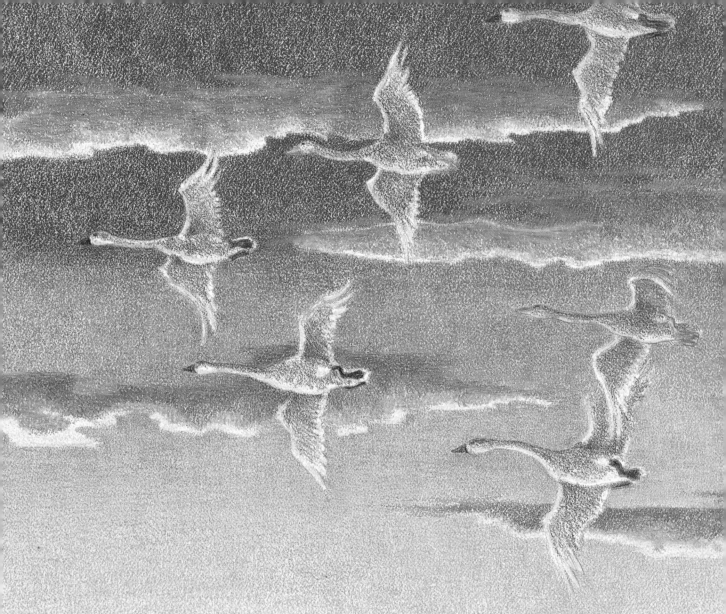

Father swan leads his family into the air. With other tundra swan families following, he turns south. The fall migration begins.

Through long days and nights, too, the swans fly far —
as many as a thousand miles — before stopping to rest
and feed. They hurry to stay ahead of winter's ice.

Finally, in late November, the flock reaches its winter home on Chesapeake Bay. At last the autumn migration has ended. Now the swans will feast on the rich plants in the bay.

Then, as winter ends, spring warmth will once again send the swans northward on their familiar flyway to their summer tundra home.

About the Tundra Swan

Also known as the whistling swan because of its high-pitched call, the tundra swan is one of only two swan species native to North America. Over four feet long and weighing about 15 pounds, with a wingspan of up to five and one-half feet, tundra swans feed on vegetation in shallow water, often tipping their tails up and stretching their long necks to reach plants on the bottom. Near the turn of this century tundra swans were in danger of becoming extinct and might have disappeared forever had it not been for the passage of the Migratory Bird Treaty Act of 1918. Now protected, so that future generations will be able to enjoy them, they currently number about 150,000 birds. Like other swans, tundra swans mate for life, fiercely defend their cygnets, and exhibit some of the strongest family bonds found in the bird world.

Glossary

Chesapeake Bay: a large inlet from the Atlantic Ocean, bordered by the states of Maryland and Virginia and fed by fresh water from a number of rivers, principally the Potomac and the Susquehanna.

cottongrass: a kind of sedge with tufted spikes.

cygnets: young swans.

hummock: a small, low, dome-shaped hill made up of rock, earth, etc.

intruder: one who enters without permission or welcome.

meltwater: water formed by melting ice.

migration: movement from one region or climate to another.

poppies: plants with showy flowers.

sedges: tufted marsh plants.

tundra: a level or nearly level treeless plain with a permanently frozen subsoil.

Points of Interest in this Book

pp. 4-5 Cygnets stay with their parents until the following breeding season.

pp. 18-19 Tundra swans nest at least a mile from each other and do not welcome visitors.